# Canadian Rockies
## Where Eagles Soar

*To my parents,*
*who showed me the beauty of the mountains*

Cirrus Publishing
P.O. Box 2879
Banff, Alberta T0L 0C0
Phone (403) 762-3134

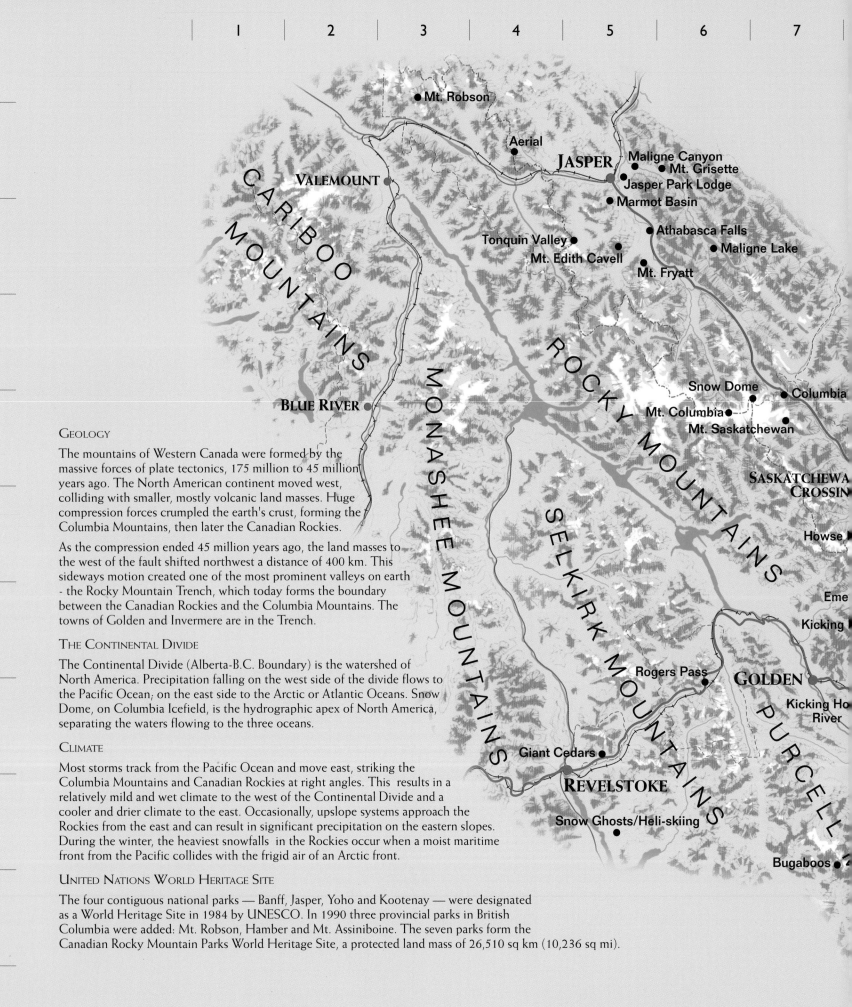

| | 1 | 2 | 3 | 4 | 5 | 6 | 7 |

Mt. Robson

Aerial

**JASPER**

Maligne Canyon

Mt. Grisette

Jasper Park Lodge

**VALEMOUNT**

Marmot Basin

Athabasca Falls

Tonquin Valley

Maligne Lake

Mt. Edith Cavell

Mt. Fryatt

CARIBOO MOUNTAINS

ROCKY MOUNTAINS

MONASHEE MOUNTAINS

Snow Dome

Columbia

Mt. Columbia

**BLUE RIVER**

Mt. Saskatchewan

SELKIRK MOUNTAINS

**SASKATCHEWAN CROSSIN**

### GEOLOGY

The mountains of Western Canada were formed by the
massive forces of plate tectonics, 175 million to 45 million
years ago. The North American continent moved west,
colliding with smaller, mostly volcanic land masses. Huge
compression forces crumpled the earth's crust, forming the
Columbia Mountains, then later the Canadian Rockies.

As the compression ended 45 million years ago, the land masses to
the west of the fault shifted northwest a distance of 400 km. This
sideways motion created one of the most prominent valleys on earth
- the Rocky Mountain Trench, which today forms the boundary
between the Canadian Rockies and the Columbia Mountains. The
towns of Golden and Invermere are in the Trench.

Howse

Eme

Kicking

### THE CONTINENTAL DIVIDE

The Continental Divide (Alberta-B.C. Boundary) is the watershed of
North America. Precipitation falling on the west side of the divide flows to
the Pacific Ocean; on the east side to the Arctic or Atlantic Oceans. Snow
Dome, on Columbia Icefield, is the hydrographic apex of North America,
separating the waters flowing to the three oceans.

Rogers Pass

**GOLDEN**

Kicking Ho
River

PURCELL

### CLIMATE

Most storms track from the Pacific Ocean and move east, striking the
Columbia Mountains and Canadian Rockies at right angles. This results in a
relatively mild and wet climate to the west of the Continental Divide and a
cooler and drier climate to the east. Occasionally, upslope systems approach the
Rockies from the east and can result in significant precipitation on the eastern slopes.
During the winter, the heaviest snowfalls in the Rockies occur when a moist maritime
front from the Pacific collides with the frigid air of an Arctic front.

Giant Cedars

**REVELSTOKE**

Snow Ghosts/Heli-skiing

Bugaboos

### UNITED NATIONS WORLD HERITAGE SITE

The four contiguous national parks — Banff, Jasper, Yoho and Kootenay — were designated
as a World Heritage Site in 1984 by UNESCO. In 1990 three provincial parks in British
Columbia were added: Mt. Robson, Hamber and Mt. Assiniboine. The seven parks form the
Canadian Rocky Mountain Parks World Heritage Site, a protected land mass of 26,510 sq km (10,236 sq mi).

A

B

C

D

E

F

G

H

I

Waterfowl Lakes

Peyto Lake

Takakkaw Falls

Herbert Lake

Skoki Lodge

Lake Louise Ski Resort

**LAKE LOUISE**

O'Hara

Moraine Lake

Castle Mtn.

Johnston Canyon

Mt. Norquay

Vermilion Pass

**BANFF**

Cycling

**COCHRANE**

Sulphur Mtn. Gondola

**CANMORE**

Trans Canada Highway

**CALGARY**

Sunshine Village

**EXSHAW**

Kananaskis Village

Mt. Assiniboine

Buller Pond

Ranch Country

Chester Lake Area

Spillway Lake

**RADIUM HOT SPRINGS**

**INVERMERE**

**FAIRMONT HOT SPRINGS**

*Bow Lake with the Icefields Parkway and Num-Ti-Jah Lodge.*

*Dusk over the Trans-Canada
Highway between Banff
and Calgary.*

›› *Dwarfing the neighbouring
peaks, Mt. Assiniboine,
3618 m (11,872 ft) is
on the Continental Divide
southwest of Banff.*

# ACKNOWLEDGMENTS

## Canadian Rockies: Where Eagles Soar

**Photography & Writing** - Scott Rowed

**Layout & Design** - Scott Rowed, Blackbird Design

**Editing** - Holly Quan, Debra Cummings

**Production & Quality Management** - Blackbird Design

**Map/Graphic Design** - Blackbird Design and Pamela Fry

In addition to the above people, the author gratefully acknowledges the assistance of the following:

ANECDOTES AND FACTUAL INFORMATION – Willy Pfisterer, Toni Klettl, Peter Sherrington, Hal Morrison and John Kellas.
I would also like to thank the contributors who wished to remained anonymous. Space limitations prevented the use of all material provided,
but I extend my sincere thanks to those who took the time to write their stories.

HELICOPTERS AND AIRPLANES (AERIAL PHOTOGRAPHY) – Alpine Helicopters (Canmore),
Yellowhead Helicopters (Valemount), Dan Bowen (Jasper).

HELI-HIKING AND HELI-SKIING – Canadian Mountain Holidays, Bugaboos; Selkirk Tangiers Helicopter Skiing.

MODELS – Skiers: John A. MacLean, John Mellis and Trevor Petersen; Mountain bikers: Rob Healy and Bruce Stephen; Climbers: Sabine Pachmayr
and Chris Ratcliffe; Cowboys: James Goin, Marc Ledwidge and Cindy Anderson; Native boy: Peter Olney; Golf: Michael Smith.

OTHER – Jennifer Lee and Blake O'Brian from Skoki Lodge, Andrea Moberg from Sulphur Mountain Gondola, and
fellow photographer Lyle Korytar who was with me on several shoots. Two shots were taken on location with RAP Films from Calgary.

I am grateful to James Dakin of London Drugs (NE Calgary) and
Mona Creasy of The Lab in Calgary for their reliable and accurate slide film processing.

Ken Uyeda and Ken Wong from Blackbird Design were most helpful with their expertise in design and production.

Throughout the project my family provided encouragement, moral support and valuable ideas.
Warm thanks go to my mother Genevieve Rowed, my sister Daphne Richard and my wife Welcy.
My daughters Kylie and Genevieve have been faithful companions to me while photographing scenery and wildlife.

# PUBLICATION INFORMATION

Canadian Cataloguing in Publication Data
Scott Rowed, 1948 -
Canadian Rockies
ISBN 0-9699546-0-3

1. Rocky Mountains, Canadian (B.C. and Alta.) – Pictorial works.* 2. Rocky Mountains, Canadian (B.C. and Alta.)*
3.Columbia Mountains (B.C.) – Pictorial works. 4. Columbia Mountains (B.C.). I. Title.
FC219.R68 1995   917.1104'4   C95-910472-0
F1090.R68 1995

Colour separations & Lithography: Friesen Printers                    Produced and printed in Western Canada

# Canadian Rockies

## Where Eagles Soar

# INTRODUCTION

About 30,000 years ago, during a time of mild climate between Ice Ages, tribes trekked from Asia to Alaska on a land bridge that joined the two continents. These early North Americans would almost certainly have seen the mountains we now call the Canadian Rockies, probably living and hunting throughout this mountainous region. Then, 20,000 years ago, the return of the Ice Age erased all evidence of these prehistoric inhabitants. Huge continental ice sheets advanced relentlessly from the far north. Mountain glaciers in the Canadian Rockies expanded to fill the valleys deep with ice, grinding away at the mountains themselves. The advancing ice forced humans to live and hunt in an ice-free corridor just east of the mountains.

The great glaciers receded once again about 11,500 years ago. Forests, wildlife and people returned to the Rockies, to a landscape much altered by glaciation. Recent archeological digs show that humans occupied the Bow Valley 11,000 years ago. For thousands of years people lived in the these mountains, hunting, fishing and gathering. Trade routes were established through the mountains between the tribes of the Kootenay region of British Columbia and the Plains tribes to the east.

Little changed until Europeans arrived. The vast open prairie was fenced into ranches and plowed into farms. The thundering herds of bison were silenced. The Native populations were decimated by smallpox. There were also many changes in mountain country, with the establishment of towns, mines and logging. In 1871 British Columbia promised to join the new Confederation of Canada, if in return Canada would build a railway linking east and west. The result was the Canadian Pacific Railway (CPR).

Construction of the CPR succeeded not only in forging a nation, but was instrumental in creating our national parks system; the railway required paying passengers, and national parks were the perfect tourist attraction. The railroad's last spike was driven at Craigellachie, B.C. in November 1885. Within days, land was set aside surrounding Sulphur Mountain's hot springs near Banff — Canada's first national park. The CPR quickly established a series of hotels: a chalet at Lake Louise (forerunner of the Chateau Lake Louise), Mt. Stephen House in Field, B.C., Glacier House at Rogers Pass and the grandest of all — the Banff Springs Hotel.

The concept of preservation as a national parks objective came much later. Conflict between nature and tourism continues, with strongly-held opinions on both sides. Nevertheless, without the CPR, establishment of the mountain national parks may not have happened for years — possibly too late to save these valleys from development.

Today, visitors to the Canadian Rockies and the neighbouring Columbia Mountains have more recreational choices than ever. Back-country use is virtually exploding as more people take up hiking, climbing, mountain biking and ski touring. Guiding services, mountaineering schools, avalanche courses and remote mountain lodges are becoming big business. Heli skiing and heli hiking have opened up remote areas to new markets.

Despite the growing popularity of these mountains, there are still places where little has changed for thousands of years. Where summits are yet to be climbed, where alpine meadows have never been touched by a hiker's boot. Where grizzlies, wolves and herds of woodland caribou roam free. And where eagles soar.

— Scott Rowed, February 1995

*Lake Louise with Mt. Victoria.*

12

# Banff

Hiking on the ski runs of Mystic
Ridge & Norquay affords this
stunning view of the Bow Valley
with Banff townsite and
Mt. Rundle, 2949 m (9675 ft).

In Banff National Park, humans and nature strike a delicate balance. Banff is Canada's busiest national park and contains the largest urban centre of any national park on earth. As tourism increases more facilities are built in the park — shops, hotels, restaurants, golf courses, ski lifts. More staff are needed to serve the increasing number of visitors. The town's boundaries are permanently fixed to preserve the surrounding natural environment, thus increasing the town's population density.

*Some of Banff's longtime residents show no respect for regulations against jaywalking.*

More people mean greater impacts on nature, notably wildlife. Although elk adapt relatively easily and even thrive in downtown Banff, dining on domestic flowers, hedges and the golf course greens, other species such as black bears, grizzlies and wolves try to avoid man and do not fare as well.

The Trans-Canada Highway runs through Banff National Park and road kills take a toll of animal life, although sometimes tragedy can have a silver lining. The death of a female wolf, for example, led to a better understanding of wolf society. Park wardens knew this wolf — she was white and walked with a limp, the result of a broken leg perhaps caused by a vehicle hit years before. She had survived, despite being crippled for months while her broken leg healed. Other wolves must have protected and fed her during that time.

Solving one problem can create new difficulties. To save wildlife (and motorists!) some of the highway has been fenced on both sides, causing a dramatic increase in the elk population. This in turn has contributed to the virtual disappearance of moose from the Bow Valley near Banff town site. The aspen forests are another victim, since aspen leaves are gourmet elk food. Young aspen trees have little chance of reaching maturity, and conifers are taking over.

Ironically, the highway fences have provided cunning coyotes with delicious meals of mutton. Coyotes have learned to trap bighorn sheep against the fence. Biologists have recently modified the fence hoping to prevent this behaviour.

The problems facing the mountain parks are complex and nowhere are they more urgent than in Banff. Individuals can ensure that their visit has the lowest possible impact on the natural balance. Walk on trails, not on vegetation. Keep a safe distance from wildlife — especially bears — and do not feed any animals.

Banff is a fascinating area, rich in history and activities. Rock climbers may be struggling up the vertical limestone face on Tunnel Mountain's south side. Meanwhile, a five-minute walk away, Shakespeare fans watch Hamlet at the Banff Centre, a world-renowned school for the fine arts.

*A mule deer fawn in the spring.*

*The Banff Springs Hotel Golf Course offers 27 holes in a magnificent mountain setting.*

*Overlooking the golf course and the Fairholme Range, the castle-like Banff Springs Hotel is one of Banff's most famous attractions. On the left of the photo is the Banff Centre.*

›› *The crags of Castle Mountain, 2766 m (9076 ft), are a prominent landmark on the drive from Banff to Lake Louise.*

One of Banff's busiest attractions, the Sulphur Mountain Gondola whisks visitors to the top of a ridge at 2285 m (7500 ft). The spectacular panorama from the upper terminal includes Banff town site, Lake Minnewanka and a vista of snowcapped mountains stretching from Kananaskis Country to the Lake Louise area. On the left is Cascade Mountain, 2998m (9076 ft).

*Winter dusk settles over Banff. On the right is the Banff Springs Hotel.*

The trails of Johnston Canyon take the hiker right into the depths of the canyon. There are seven waterfalls, ranging up to 30 m (100 ft) high.

The Stoney, Salish and Kootenay tribes have all lived in the Bow Valley at various times. Visitors can learn more about native culture and history at the Luxton Museum in Banff or by attending powwows. This boy from the Yakima tribe in Washington State was photographed during a powwow on the Stoney Reserve between Banff and Calgary.

# URSUS INTERRUPTUS

The ground was soft and dry and fragrant lodgepole pines afforded us privacy from the highway. We spread our blanket, uncorked a bottle of champagne, and munched on cheese and crackers. It was a magical time of talk, laughter, and sharing...and well...things just happened, as often does between couples feeling free and...loving.

Moments later I heard a sound and peered up from our cosy blanket. Beady brown eyes gazed back at me curiously. I laughed and announced, "Claudio, there's a huge black bear sniffing at us." Claudio panicked. He tossed our leftover food and champagne toward the bear to distract it. We held the blanket around us and backed away slowly. I focused my attention so intently on the bear that I hardly noticed when Claudio ran up the hill towards our car — leaving me behind! "Run!" he yelled.

As I scampered through the trees dragging the blanket, I could hear the bear chasing me, coming closer. I was certain that this would be the end of me. Claudio threw a large rock — just missing me — but fortunately scaring the bear back to our food and clothing.

We nestled against the car with nothing but our blanket. Unfortunately the keys were in my shoe — with the bear! After a few minutes a station wagon drove up. Eight small children peered curiously and asked their father, "Daddy, why don't they have any clothes on?"

"There's a warden station ten minutes ahead," I said. "Please tell the warden to help us." Forty-five minutes passed. The sun was dropping and a chill filled the air. We flagged down another car. The couple stared for an eternity before talking to us. I explained our situation and asked them to make sure the warden was coming soon. Claudio then nudged me and pointed. The bear was running up the hill toward us! Hastily we clambered into the back seat of our rescuer's car.

*Grizzly in a thicket of buffalo berries.*

After a five-minute drive down the highway, we saw the warden truck, with lights flashing, speeding toward us. We waved it down, then sheepishly tiptoed across the highway with nothing but our blanket and our embarrassment.

When the warden stopped laughing he took his gun, his dog, and Claudio — in a pair of borrowed shorts — to retrieve our scattered, torn clothing. The bear, probably drunk, scurried up a tree with the champagne bottle and one of my tasty suede shoes clamped firmly in his mouth.

Driving home to Banff with one bare foot was no problem — much easier than filling in the report. "You need my name?" I moaned. Weeks later the local Banff paper, The Crag and Canyon, got wind of this story, but thankfully they left out our names.

— Anonymous contribution

*To travel in style, try the Rocky Mountaineer. Shown here just west of Banff town site, this train operates two routes: Calgary to Vancouver, and Jasper to Vancouver. Catering to sightseers, the train travels only by daylight with an overnight stop in Kamloops, British Columbia.*

# Lake Louise

The Chateau Lake Louise in early
winter, looking to Mt. Victoria,
3464 m (11,365 ft).

No area in the Canadian Rockies offers as much variety as Lake Louise. The visitor can choose from activities as diverse as gently paddling a canoe to testing nerve and fitness by scaling cliffs and glaciers. Hiking, horseback riding, shopping and fine dining are to be found here too. When the winter snow falls, the downhill and cross-country skiing are both excellent. Other visitors prefer skating in front of the Chateau, or horse-drawn sleigh rides to the end of the lake.

The Lake Louise area has a grand tradition of climbing and mountain guiding. In 1896, the first fatality in North American mountaineering occurred when American Philip Abbot fell to his death during a first-ascent attempt on Mt. Lefroy. Nearby Abbot Pass carries his name. The next summer his climbing partner, Charles Fay, teamed up with others for another attempt. This time, however, they hired the services of a Swiss guide. This climb, and several others, were successful and safe.

In 1899 the CPR hired Swiss mountain guides to take Chateau guests to the nearby summits in safety. This service continued until 1955, when the contract with the last two guides expired. As a tribute to the skill and professionalism of the Swiss guides, there was not a single serious climbing injury during that time.

Lake Louise is an important training ground for young climbers today. At the west end of Lake Louise are steep quartzite cliffs, overhanging in places, a favourite spot for local climbers. In winter, these climbers swap their rock shoes and chalk bags for crampons and ice tools to tackle a frozen waterfall beside the cliff.

Hiking is wonderful in the Louise area. The most heavily used trails are those closest to Lake Louise and Moraine Lake. Hikes to the Plain of the Six Glaciers and Lake Agnes each reward hikers with an alpine tea house! Larch Valley above Moraine Lake is especially popular when the larch trees turn golden in September.

*The delicate calypso orchid (Calypso bulbosa) grows profusely on shady forest floors during the early summer.*

On more remote trails in the area a hiker may spend the entire day without seeing another person.

The Lake Louise ski area operates a chairlift for summer visitors. The spectacular view includes all the major peaks of the Louise area as well as many to the west in Yoho National Park. On a clear day the steep, symmetrical peak of Mt. Assiniboine, 72 km (45 mi) to the southeast, is a distinctive feature on the skyline.

*A couple canoeing on Herbert Lake, a short drive north of Lake Louise.*

Moraine Lake and the Valley of the Ten Peaks, after an overnight dusting of snow. This famous view is only a five-minute walk from the parking lot.

*Larch needles swirling in a whirlpool of a mountain creek. The needles of Lyall's larch turn golden in mid-September but within ten days have faded and fallen. Visitors planning for this short "larch season" should try September 18 to 21, but this can vary a few days.*

*Larches line the shore of Myosotis Lake, near Skoki Lodge, a popular backcountry destination for hikers and cross-country skiers.*

*The Lake Louise Ski Area combines spectacular mountain scenery with excellent skiing. Here an expert skier takes "air" in the back bowls.*

*Sunrise at Lake Louise.*

*The friendly gray jays are seen frequently in the Canadian Rockies, especially during picnics!*

## SOUP CAN BINOCULARS

It was hunting season and I was on boundary patrol in the northern part of Jasper National Park. My job was to make sure that hunters didn't sneak into the park to shoot the animals. I climbed Sunset Peak on the park boundary and trained my binoculars on the next valley where I knew of two hunting parties. I spotted them and I was sure they could see me on the mountaintop. Above the hunters was a herd of caribou — in the park.

I wanted to be sure they would continue to see me so they wouldn't be tempted to poach. But I had a full day's ride ahead of me, so I couldn't stay. Instead I placed two soup cans on the boundary cairn and aimed them like binoculars into the hunting

country. Beside these "binoculars", I angled two lids to reflect morning and evening sunlight onto the cans. Then I returned to my horses and rode away, hoping my trick would work.

It did. Later that winter I met the hunting guide from one of the parties. "Klettl!" he demanded. "Is that all you wardens have to do? Just lie around in the sun all day and watch hunters?" It wasn't until years later that I told him the truth.

— Toni Klettl, retired park warden

*Park warden patrol at Ptarmigan Lake in the Skoki area.*

# The Icefields Parkway

*Peyto Lake's rich blue colour is typical of glacier-fed lakes in the Canadian Rockies. Glaciers high on the mountains slowly flow into the valleys. This moving ice grinds away the bedrock forming a flour, or glacial silt. Streams from the melting glaciers carry this silt, which refracts sunlight to give lakes and rivers this remarkable colour.*

The roadway known as the Icefields Parkway, connecting Lake Louise and the town of Jasper, winds through some of the Canadian Rockies' most impressive scenery. The road climbs over two high passes — Bow and Sunwapta — and skirts the shores of colourful mountain lakes. Sheep, bears, elk, goats and deer are abundant. The dramatic cliffs, glaciers and jagged summits are a constantly changing panorama of colour and contrast.

*With their huge tires and low gearing, SnoCoaches travel across the Athabasca Glacier with ease. Each summer over 400,000 visitors take this unique ride.*

Visitors can park right at the toe of the Athabasca Glacier, one of eight valley glaciers flowing from the main body of the Columbia Icefield. Visible above the steep cliffs is a thick layer of ice like icing on a giant cake. This is the rim of the Columbia Icefield. Most of the Icefield sits on an extensive plateau above 3000 m (10,000 ft), surrounded by many of the highest mountains in the Canadian Rockies.

These tall peaks block moist storms heading eastward from the Pacific Ocean, forcing the moist air to rise and release huge amounts of snow onto the Icefield. The short, cool summers melt only a fraction of this snow, so each winter the snow accumulates on top of unmelted snow from previous years. Resembling annual growth rings on trees, these annual snow layers are visible on the higher glaciers where the ice has cracked, revealing a cross section.

Under the massive weight of accumulated snow, the lower layers compress into ice and flow into the valleys. If the forward flow of the glacier exceeds the summer melt at the glacier's toe, the glacier advances. During the past 100 years, however, glaciers in the Rockies have receded.

Glaciers, while beautiful, are dangerous territory. Surface cracks called crevasses are deep, narrow, and frequently hidden by thin snow bridges. Only experienced mountaineers with the right equipment should venture alone onto the treacherous ice. For visitors, icewalks led by professional mountain guides are available. Boots, crampons and warm clothing are provided.

The Columbia Icefield area is a hiker's paradise. Because of this region's altitude, hikers have quick access to high alpine terrain. A short walk up the Parker Ridge trail offers a spectacular panoramic view over the Saskatchewan Glacier, the largest valley glacier flowing from the Columbia Icefield. Mountain goats are common near the top of Parker Ridge, especially on the south side.

Without stopping, the Icefields Parkway can be driven in about two hours from Lake Louise to Jasper. A rushed trip, however, seems almost sinful. There is so much to see, and the mountains look different with every change of weather or season — even locals make this drive a full-day event.

*Straddling the Continental Divide along the western edge of the Columbia Icefield, the summit of Mt. Columbia is the highest point in Alberta at 3747 m (12,294 ft). In the Canadian Rockies, Mt. Columbia is second in height only to Mt. Robson.*

*Wild strawberries* (Fragaria glauca) *are plentiful through the Canadian Rockies, but do not get caught with red stains on your fingers and lips. Picking berries is against national park regulations.*

*Canoeists explore the Upper Waterfowl Lake, against the spectacular backdrop of Stairway Peak, 2999 m (9840 ft). Moose are common along the shoreline.*

*›› The clouds part after a winter storm to reveal the steep cliffs and glaciers of Howse Peak, 3290 m (10,793 ft), near Waterfowl Lakes.*

*Hikers hear the high-pitched cry of the pika long before seeing one of these skittish little rock rabbits, which live in boulder fields. Pikas spend their summers constantly gathering vegetation for food during the long winter.*

*The smooth white cliffs of Mt. Wilson, 3240 m (10,700 ft), tower above the Icefields Parkway near Saskatchewan Crossing.*

*Battle scars of the rut. The fight for supremacy and breeding rights have left this bighorn ram with shredded horns and a cut above his nose.*

*The Athabasca Glacier with the Columbia Icefield Visitors' Centre. The peak on the left is Mt. Andromeda, 3444 m (11,300 ft). Snow Dome, 3457 m (11,340 ft), is on the right.*

*Ice climbing in the Columbia Icefield area.*

›› *Wind blasting over Snow Dome forms thin clouds as warmer air cools on the Icefield surface. Snow Dome is the hydrographic apex of North America, supplying water to three oceans — the Pacific, Arctic and Atlantic via Hudson Bay. On the left is Mt. Columbia. Scientists studying glaciers can learn what the earth's climate was like hundreds of years ago. Air bubbles trapped in the ice show us how the atmosphere has changed over time.*

*The moon setting over Mt. Saskatchewan, 3342 m (10,964 ft), at sunrise. This view is from the Icefields Parkway south of the Columbia Icefield.*

*The yellow mountain avens (Dryas drummondii) is a common flower on gravel beds.*

# Jasper

*Nestled among high glacial peaks,*
*Maligne Lake is the largest natural*
*lake in the Canadian Rockies with*
*a length of 22 km (14 mi).*
*Tour boats take visitors to this*
*famous view of Spirit Island.*

*Columbine* (Aquilegia flavescens).

Hundreds of lakes, high glaciated mountains, flower-studded alpine meadows, abundant wildlife, deep canyons, waterfalls, hot springs and even sand dunes — Jasper National Park embodies all this and more. With 10,878 sq km (4200 sq mi), Jasper is by far the largest of Canada's mountain national parks. Extensive remote areas are rarely visited, allowing wildlife to thrive unaffected by man.

Five of the Canadian Rockies' ten highest peaks lie within the borders of this extensive park. All five of these giants are in the Columbia Icefield area, including Mt. Columbia, the second-highest peak in the Canadian Rockies at 3747 m (12,294 ft).

Throughout Jasper National Park, hikers and sightseers have easy access to high alpine areas. The upper terminal of the Jasper Tramway, on The Whistlers mountain, is above treeline and provides unobstructed views of Jasper town site, a multitude of colourful lakes, and glaciated peaks from the Maligne Lake area in the southeast to Mt. Robson in the northwest.

A hike in the Cavell Meadows area presents a rich mixture of lakes, flowers and dramatic views to Mt. Edith Cavell and the Angel Glacier. The trail skirts a lateral moraine deposited by the Cavell Glacier, and continues all the way to the glacier itself. Occasionally, chunks of ice split from the glacier to become icebergs floating in Cavell Pond.

The Maligne area is a must! Maligne Canyon is the deepest and longest gorge in the Canadian Rockies. Medicine Lake drains through sink holes on the lake bottom; water flows through underground rivers into Maligne Canyon and to springs near Jasper town site. Each autumn, Medicine Lake completely disappears leaving only braided streams through the mud flats.

Besides taking a cruise boat on Maligne Lake, there are numerous other rewarding activities in the area. Trail rides or hikes into the Bald Hills offer superb views of Maligne Lake and the surrounding mountains. Commercial whitewater rafting operators offer trips on the Maligne River downstream from the lake. In winter, cross-country skiing is popular, and ski tourers enjoy long powder runs in the Bald Hills.

Bighorn sheep thrive in the open areas east of Jasper town site. Nearby Miette Hot Springs is the hottest of the developed hot springs in the Canadian Rockies.

The town of Jasper has maintained a quiet charm. More isolated than Banff, Jasper has a stable population base and a strong sense of community. While tourism employs many people in the town, other industries such as petroleum and transportation diversify the economy.

Jasper is a friendly town in a magnificent setting.

*The Maligne River plunges into the depths of Maligne Canyon. After the last ice age ended 11,000 years ago, the river began cutting into the limestone resulting in a narrow gorge that today is up to 55 m (180 ft) deep. The canyon is so narrow that falling boulders have wedged between the walls. In winter, guided hikes provide a glimpse into the eerie world of frozen waterfalls at the bottom of the canyon.*

*Although there are higher falls in the Rockies, the large volume of water gives Athabasca Falls tremendous power. There are fenced walkways on all sides of the Falls, offering good views. Nonetheless, several people have died by venturing beyond the fence and falling from the slippery rock.*

*The Jasper Park Lodge with Lac Beauvert and the golf course. Dozens of picturesque lakes colour the landscape of the wide Athabasca Valley near Jasper. The mountains in the background are the Colin Range.*

*Flutings in the snow on a ridge near Mt. Fryatt. These narrow snow
gullies are caused by frequent avalanches over steep rock.*

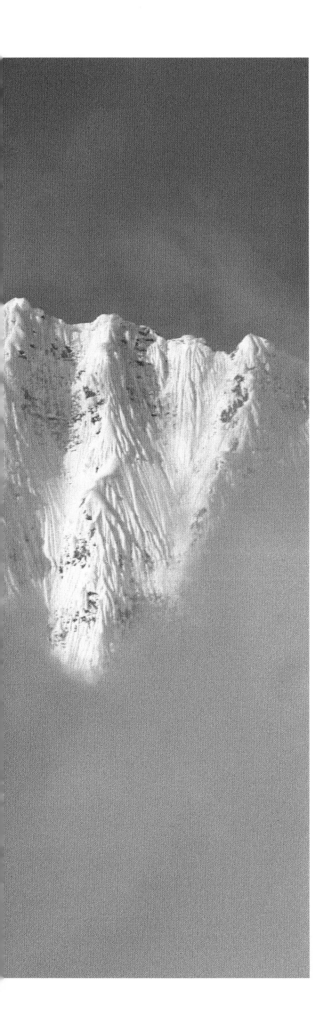

*Marmot Basin ski area near Jasper offers terrific powder snow in both
the high alpine terrain and the lower tree-flanked runs.*

›› *The Ramparts form a striking backdrop to Amethyst Lakes
in Jasper Park's most famous back-country destination,
the Tonquin Valley. This area is accessible only by foot or horseback.
Despite the high elevation, the fishing is excellent. Hikers frequently see a
herd of caribou grazing near Maccarib Pass.*

*A white-tailed ptarmigan out for an afternoon stroll. Thriving in the higher elevations, this bird is a master of camouflage. Pure white in the winter, it turns speckled brown during the summer.*

*Sunlight through storm clouds provides stark contrast on Mt. Grisette in the Colin Range.*

*›› Forest-fire smoke fills the valleys west of Jasper in this aerial view. On the left is Mt. Edith Cavell and on the right are the Ramparts of the Tonquin Valley.*

*A common sight in rockslides and moraines is the hoary marmot, nicknamed "whistling" marmot because of its piercing call. Jasper's ski resort, Marmot Basin, and The Whistlers mountain (Jasper Tramway) both derive their names from this member of the woodchuck family.*

# FIRST ASCENT PEAK

"I want to climb Mt. Edith Cavell," announced the tourist.

Willy Pfisterer, an experienced and wise Austrian mountain guide, glanced at the man's protruding stomach. Willy had climbed Cavell many times and knew it to be a long, arduous ascent. "What have you climbed before?" he inquired.

"I've climbed the Matterhorn!" the man replied.

"When was that?"

"Twenty years ago."

"Cavell is dangerous right now — too much snow," said Willy. "But I know of a smaller mountain in the Colin Range. It looks like super rock climbing, but it's never been climbed. We could make a first ascent!" The man agreed.

Since the two climbers were roped up and belaying each other, Willy arrived first on the summit. Confronting him was a cairn — a pile of rocks constructed by other climbers to mark the summit.

Quickly he stuffed the summit register into his rucksack and scattered the rocks from the cairn. A few minutes later the tourist joined him, out of breath but excited and proud.

"Congratulations!" said Willy, shaking the man's hand. "What is your wife's name?"

"Elizabeth."

"Then I name this peak 'Mt. Elizabeth'!" Willy announced. "Help me build a cairn and we'll leave a record of our ascent."

After the man had safely rappelled from the summit Willy hastily returned the original summit register before descending.

— Willy Pfisterer, Mountain Guide

*The north face of Mt. Edith Cavell, 3363 m (11,033 ft), with alpine flowers. The excellent trails through Cavell Meadows offer some of the most enjoyable hiking in the Canadian Rockies.*

# Kananaskis

*Sunset reflection of the Opal Range*
*on Spillway Lake.*

Sprawling over 4000 sq km (1000 sq mi) of the Rockies southeast of Banff National Park, Kananaskis Country is a relative newcomer to the recreation scene. In the 1980s the Alberta government created this mountain playground as an alternative to the increasingly busy national parks. The Kananaskis area today includes a luxury hotel complex, two 18-hole golf courses, about 20 campgrounds and an extensive network of hiking, equestrian and bicycle trails. Downhill skiers can choose between Fortress Mountain and Nakiska. The latter area was developed to host the 1988 Winter Olympics' alpine ski events. The nearby Canmore Nordic Centre was built for the Olympic cross-country ski races.

Situated on the drier eastern slopes of the Rockies, K-Country has extensive areas of grassland and open forest. This excellent wildlife habitat is also used for cattle grazing. Flower species grow here that are not found in the wetter climates to the west. Heli hiking, not allowed in the national parks, is a thriving business in the Canmore area.

Highway 40, K-Country's main artery, reaches an elevation of 2206 m (7237 ft) at Highwood Pass and is the highest paved road in Canada. At this elevation the highway enters the realm of alpine larch trees. Normally found far above a major roadway, larches — with their spectacular golden September colour — here grow adjacent to Highway 40.

Climbing steeply from Canmore, the Smith-Dorrien Highway is K-Country's other main access. This wide gravel road passes beside Spray Lakes and joins Highway 40 near Lower Kananaskis Lake. The Smith-Dorrien region is a favourite for hiking, fishing and ski touring. Mt. Engadine Lodge, just south of Spray Lakes,

*Bald eagles (above) and golden eagles can be seen throughout the Canadian Rockies. Spring and fall are especially exciting in the eastern slopes of the Rockies when 6000 to 7000 eagles, mostly golden eagles, migrate between the Arctic and the American Rockies. The birds fly north to the Yukon and Alaska — possibly even to Siberia. Soaring in updrafts above the mountain ridges, they glide at speeds up to 180 km/h (110 mph) without even flapping their wings. This spectacular migration was first discovered in 1992 by Peter Sherrington of Cochrane.*

offers overnight accommodation and gourmet meals. Hikers destined for Mt. Assiniboine Provincial Park in British Columbia usually start their journey from the Spray Lakes area, or fly from Canmore by helicopter.

Numerous recreational opportunities make K-Country a welcome addition to tourism in the Alberta Rockies.

*Sunset at Buller Pond, a popular fishing and picnic stop beside the Smith-Dorrien Highway. Forest fires in British Columbia filled the air with smoke, turning the sky crimson.*

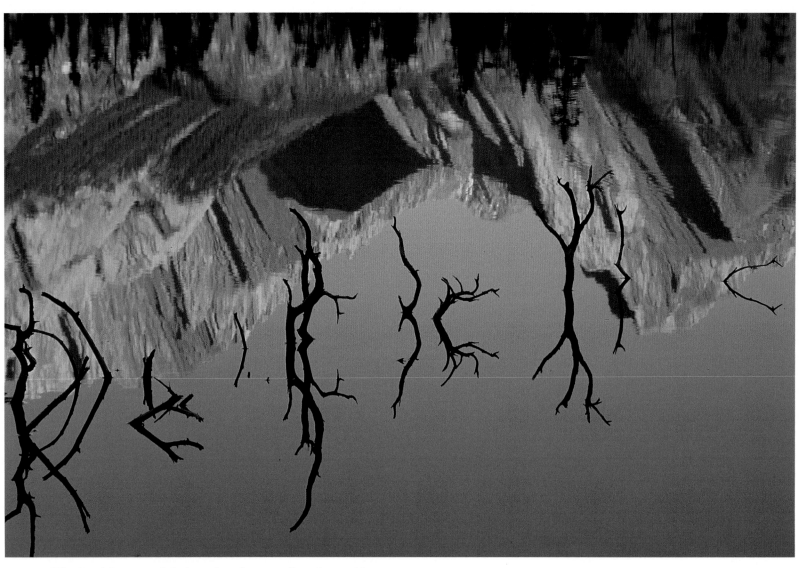

The Opal Range and the branches of a partially submerged log are
reflected in Spillway Lake.

Vast alpine meadows are common through K-Country. These fleabanes
were growing among scattered larch trees near Chester Lake.

*Blowing in the wind, these wildflowers — paintbrush, valerian and columbine — are in the Kananaskis Range of Peter Lougheed Provincial Park. Winter avalanches cleared the trees to create this lush alpine garden.*

*Grizzly bears spend their summer months grubbing for food to fatten themselves for their long winter dormancy. Most of their diet is vegetarian — roots and berries. Grizzlies generally try to avoid contact with man, but each bear is different and somewhat unpredictable. Attacks do occur, especially if the bear senses a threat to cubs or food. Note the long claws. The teeth are also impressive. To avoid bear encounters, hikers should frequently make noise thus alerting bears to their presence.*

Kananaskis Village overlooks the golf courses along the Kananaskis River. Towering above the village on the right is Mt. Kidd at 2958 m (9704 ft). Fortress Mountain Ski Resort is in the distance on the left.

After an autumn snowfall, mountain bikers ride the crest of a ridge near Canmore. The lenticular clouds signify strong winds at high elevations.

In southern Alberta, mothers do let their babies grow up to be cowboys. Horses are still used daily on ranches as tools of the trade. K-Country maintains five equestrian campgrounds and over 200 km (125 mi) of the most spectacular equestrian trails in Canada.

With grasslands and open forests, the foothills southwest of Calgary are ranch country. On this September morning, the aspen trees are changing colour and the first snow has already fallen at higher elevations.

# Yoho and Kootenay National Parks

*The Lake O'Hara area of Yoho
National Park is a hiker's dream
with an extensive network of trails,
thoughtfully planned to offer the most
rewarding views. On this brilliant
September day, the golden Lyall's
larches on the Opabin Plateau
contrast with the cobalt sky behind
Mt. Huber, 3368 m (11,051 ft).*

oho is a Cree word meaning "it is wonderful". For Canada's second-oldest national park, with its towering peaks, extensive glaciers, thundering waterfalls and pristine lakes, Yoho is a fitting name.

The glacier-fed waters of Takakkaw Falls in the Little Yoho Valley cascade 380 m (1246 ft) over a spectacular limestone cliff. At the base of the falls, accessible by a short trail from the parking area, Takakkaw's tremendous power is visible, audible — and shakes the ground.

In winter, deep snow closes the Takakkaw access road. The crowds have gone, many animals are hibernating, and even Takakkaw Falls is still and quiet, a frozen tower of ice clinging to the rock wall. Human visitors now travel on skis. Some are climbers tackling the vertical ice, but most are skiers seeking powder snow on Mt. Field or on the expansive glaciers of the Little Yoho Valley.

Just across the Trans-Canada Highway from the Little Yoho lies another pristine valley, the Lake O'Hara area. Here is a varied landscape, a myriad of lakes among precipitous cliffs and glaciers. The Lake O'Hara area is the opposite (west) side of the mountain chains visible from Lake Louise and Moraine Lake.

Farther west lies Emerald Lake, a true gem. The Emerald Lake Lodge, open all year, is possibly the most peaceful, romantic getaway in the Rockies. Across the lake from the Lodge is the rugged President Range; behind the Lodge is Mt. Burgess. The Burgess Shale is world renowned among geologists for exquisitely preserved fossils — a snapshot of bizarre life forms of the Cambrian era, 530 million years ago.

Bordering Yoho Park to the southeast is Kootenay National Park. Like Banff Park, Kootenay owes its park status to a hot spring, in this case Radium Hot Springs. Unlike Banff, Jasper or Yoho,

*In midsummer elk antlers are in soft velvet.*

Kootenay National Park has no town within its borders. Most of the land in Kootenay Park is relatively undisturbed. Bears are commonly seen beside the highway, and mountain goats often feed along the exposed clay banks near Kootenay Crossing.

From arduous hikes to the total relaxation of a hot-spring soak, Kootenay offers just about everything a visitor could desire.

*Surface hoar crystals shroud a dead spruce tree near Vermilion Pass. Unlike snow, which falls from the sky, surface hoar forms like cold-temperature dew. During clear weather moisture condenses onto trees, bushes and the snow surface. Although beautiful to see, back-country skiers note surface hoar with caution because it creates a weak, slippery layer deep in the snowpack. The resulting avalanche danger can persist for several weeks and is difficult to predict.*

*The Kicking Horse River downstream from Yoho Park affords the Rockies' most exciting white-water rafting. Several companies offer professionally guided trips.*

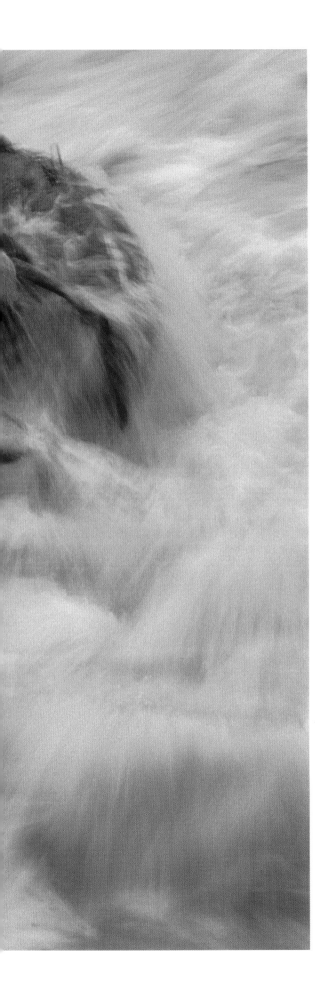

*The simple-stemmed twisted-stalk (Streptopus roseus) grows in moist forests.*

Late afternoon sun adds a warm glow to the snowfields and peaks of Kootenay National Park and Mt. Assiniboine Provincial Park. This photo is taken from the Sunshine Village Ski Resort.

The Lake O'Hara Lodge, with the spectacular backdrop of Mt. Hungabee, 3493 m (11,457 ft), Ringrose Peak, 3281 m (10,765 ft) and Mt. Lefroy, 3423 m (11,230 ft). Odaray Prospect, one of O'Hara's hiking circuits, was closed indefinitely in 1993 because of human/grizzly incidents. Wildlife biologists have found that local grizzlies dine on tasty goat meat. Nothing can catch the agile mountain goat on steep rock, but biologists suspect that lush meadow grass may entice goats to stray from the safety of the cliff. A grizzly could then cut a goat's escape route and chase it down through the open forest.

*At Kicking Horse Pass, both the Trans-Canada Highway and the CPR cross the Continental Divide between Banff National Park and Yoho National Park. The peaks to the left of the highway are Cathedral Mountain, 3189 m (10,464 ft) and Mt. Stephen, 3199 m (10,495 ft). Wapta Lake is between the highway and the railway.*

*Emerald Lake with Mt. Burgess. Summer visitors can stretch their legs on the numerous trails, or paddle leisurely around the lake. The snow-capped mountain to the right is Yoho's highest peak, Mt. Goodsir, 3562 m (11,686 ft).*

*A golden-mantled ground squirrel eating kinnikinnik berries.*

# THE WOODPILE

The winter was cold, and my friend's pile of firewood was down to the last few sticks. He remembered seeing an abundance of dry wood, sawn and split into just the right size for his fireplace. It happened to be at a nearby national park picnic site, but nobody would be there in winter.

The trunk of his car was almost full with firewood. As he was walking with an armload of wood to his car he heard an engine. Looking up, he spied a park warden's truck driving toward him. Without hesitation he turned back to the woodpile and neatly laid the wood from his arms back onto the pile. He returned to his car, took out more sticks and headed back to the woodpile.

The warden slammed the door to his truck and stormed over. "What do you think you're doing?" he demanded.

"Remember that big dump of snow last week?" my friend asked. The warden nodded.

My friend continued. "I was down here cross country skiing, but when I tried to drive back up the hill, there was too much snow for my car. So I put this wood in my trunk to give me some traction. Thank goodness it worked because it was really cold. Now that the road is plowed, I'm just returning the wood. It doesn't belong to me."

"That's very commendable," said the warden. "I wish more people were as honest as you!"

— Anonymous contribution

*Takakkaw Falls is one of the highest waterfalls in Canada.*
*Fed by the Daly Glacier, the Falls' volume increases during the afternoon*
*when the sun's heat melts more ice.*

# Mt. Robson

*From the highest summit in the
Canadian Rockies, Mt. Robson's
southwest face plunges precipitously
to one of the lowest points in the
Rockies. No other mountain wall in
the Rockies (Canadian or American)
comes close to matching this vertical
distance of 3000 m (10,000 ft). For
comparison, Mt. Victoria's summit
is 1733 m (5685 ft) above the shores
of Lake Louise. After covering that
same distance on Robson, a climber
is just approaching the overnight hut!*

M t. Robson defines its own class. At 3954 m (12,972 ft), Robson soars 207 m (678 ft) above the Canadian Rockies' next tallest peak, Mt. Columbia. By comparison, Mt. Columbia is only 201 m (658 ft) above the *eleventh* highest peak, Mt. Temple.

Many of the Canadian Rockies' giants are remote and only a few of these mountains are visible from the highways, often in distant, fleeting glimpses. Fortunately, the Yellowhead Highway passes close to Mt. Robson, offering unobstructed views (clouds permitting!) of the entire southwest face, the tallest mountain face in the Rockies.

Hikers can reap even greater rewards. An easy four-kilometre (2.5 mile) walk on a wide trail leads through lush cedar forest to Kinney Lake at Robson's base. A little farther on, waterfalls cascade from all sides of the Valley of a Thousand Falls. The trail then climbs steeply beside the Robson River, past thundering Emperor Falls, and around the northwest corner of Robson to Berg Lake. Hikers can camp at Berg Lake and make day hikes up the nearby mountains. The views from these peaks to Robson and Berg Lake rank among the most spectacular anywhere in the Canadian Rockies.

*Close-up detail of a shooting star* (Dodecatheon pauciflorum). *This delicate flower grows in wet low-lying areas.*

Robson is a magnet to mountaineers. Climbers come from around the world to test their skills and endurance on the steep rock walls, ice and snow. With binoculars, mountaineers high on the summit icefield can be seen even from the highway. Unlike many mountains, Robson offers no easy route to the summit, which is steep and exposed on all sides. Avalanches of snow or glacier ice are a constant threat to climbers. The first climbers' hut, a fibreglass igloo erected in 1966, was swept off the mountain three years later by a massive spring avalanche. Today climbers still find shattered pieces of yellow fibreglass strewn over the lower half of the mountain.

There is only one Mt. Robson.

*Morning sun glistens on Robson's north face. First climbed in 1963, this is one of the most beautiful ice faces in North America — a classic climb.*

*Situated just west of the Continental Divide, the Robson area receives generous amounts of rain and snow, creating exquisite waterfalls through moss-draped forests.*

*Reaching far above the neighbouring peaks, Robson creates its own weather. The frequent cloud caps create mounds and pinnacles of rime and snow called gargoyles. These are most pronounced along Emperor Ridge, in the top left corner of this photo. The horizontal bands in the rock led to the Indian name, "Yuh-hai-has-kun"— the "Mountain of the Spiral Road".*

*Mountain goats are abundant at higher elevations through the Robson area. One party of climbers even found goat tracks on Robson's summit!*

*Berg Lake, on Robson's north side, is named for the abundant icebergs that break off the Tumbling Glacier. The spectacular trail to this side of Robson is accessible by foot; Mt. Robson Ranch also conducts guided trail rides in the area. Helicopter tours are available from Yellowhead Helicopters in Valemount, B.C.*

*Sunset on the Emperor Face, taken from the Berg Lake Trail. This menacing wall of ice and rock was first climbed in 1978 and has seen few successful repeat ascents. Several parties intending to climb this route have abandoned their plans after their first look!*

*Climbers descending the southwest face.*

# The Columbia Mountains

*"Snow ghosts" guard a ridge in the Selkirk Mountains near Revelstoke. Moisture-laden storms from the Pacific Ocean bring enormous quantities of snow to the western side of the Columbia Mountains. By mid-winter, four to five metres (13 to 16 ft) of snow blanket the landscape. In this photo, the Columbia Valley is shrouded in cloud, a common occurrence during early winter.*

Deep, narrow valleys, large lakes, lush forests, huge winter snowfalls, extensive glaciers and granite spires. These characterize the Columbia Mountains of eastern British Columbia. Situated west of the Canadian Rockies, the Columbias include four separate ranges — the Cariboos in the northwest, the Monashees, the Selkirks, and in the southeast, the Purcells.

In the late 1800s towns and cities sprang up almost overnight in the Columbia Mountains as rich deposits of gold and silver lured fortune seekers to this remote area. Some settlements, such as Barkerville in the Cariboos and Sandon in the Selkirks, became ghost towns when the ore was gone, though many buildings and artifacts have been preserved. For several decades logging has been the region's main industry; unfortunately, trees were regarded as a virtually unlimited resource. Little consideration was given to conservation and reforestation until recently. Logging is currently an industry in decline.

Tourism, however, is on the increase. The Columbia Mountains offer superb skiing, canoeing, fishing, mountain biking, swimming, hiking and climbing. Many of today's residents came to the region to enjoy the beauty of the mountains and lakes and the casual lifestyle.

In the spring of 1965, Austrian Hans Gmoser guided a group of skiers in the Bugaboos. He had guided many ski touring parties before, but on that trip something was added that would change skiing forever — a helicopter. Only a handful of skiers experienced the first heli-ski trip. The next year there were 70 guests, then 150 in 1967. Gmoser needed a lodge but did not have the money. The clients, by then completely hooked on this new sport, financed

*Shooting stars* (Dodecatheon pauciflorum) *and glacier lilies* (Erythronium grandiflorum). *The glacier lily is one of the earliest flowers in the spring, often blooming right to the edge of the melting snow.*

the new lodge in exchange for future skiing. Today, Canadian Mountain Holidays operates from nine bases, all in the Columbia Mountains. Clients must book their ski holidays a year in advance.

Visitors with a sense of adventure and a love of nature will find the Columbia Mountains region irresistible. A word of caution — a lot of people who were "passing through" for a few days have quit their city jobs to move there!

*The clean, solid granite of the Bugaboos attracts elite climbers from around the world. Here, the last rays of the setting sun light the west buttress of the South Howser Spire, 3307 m (10,850 ft). This elegant line was first climbed in 1961 by Fred Beckey and Yvon Chouinard in a strenuous two-day effort.*

*A mule deer fawn runs at high speed across a meadow. White spots help to hide the fawn from predators when it lies still in the forest.*

‹‹ *Heavy precipitation in the Columbia Mountains creates a lush cedar-hemlock forest at lower elevations, such as this stand near the Giant Cedars Nature Trail in Mt. Revelstoke National Park. The broad-leaved plant on the right of the photo is devil's club. The stems and undersides of the leaves are lined with thousands of sharp thorns, just waiting to penetrate a hiker's skin and break off. Devil's club truly deserves its name.*

*Red monkeyflowers (Mimulus lewisii) in the Bugaboos. These showy flowers, blooming in mid August, grow prolifically beside alpine streams throughout the Columbia Mountains.*

*A climber in the Bugaboos rappels an overhang near the Conrad Kain Hut.*

The Rogers Pass section of the Trans-Canada Highway in
Glacier National Park was the most difficult and costly
highway construction project in Canada. The huge Selkirk
snowfalls, combined with steep, narrow valleys result in large
and frequent avalanches. Despite a full-time staff of snow experts
studying the snow, and a military unit to shoot down
avalanches with artillery, heavy snowfalls can still cause
highway closures.

Heli hikers with CMH Bugaboos admire the view to the Bugaboo Spires. Each day, helicopters fly clients to spectacular locations for leisurely hiking with a professional guide. In the evening hikers return to the Bugaboo Lodge, luxurious despite its remote location. This is the home of Canada's first commercial helicopter skiing.

›› A heli skier with Selkirk Tangiers Heli Skiing weaves his way through a fantasy forest of snow ghosts. The Columbia Mountains offer perhaps the greatest skiing in the world. Deep powder snow, vast glaciers, and steep, exciting tree skiing at lower elevations have spawned a heli ski industry that now supports at least 17 separate bases. In addition there are several snowcat ski companies and numerous guided ski touring companies operating from remote lodges.